SACRED THREADS

SACRED THREADS

REMEMBERING PAST LIVES, SOUL CONNECTIONS & THE ETERNAL SELF

The Sacred Space Press

The Sacred Space Press

SACRED THREADS
Remembering Past Lives, Soul Connections & the Eternal Self

Copyright © 2025 Abigail Henry

All rights reserved. No part of this publication may be copied, reproduced, stored or transmitted in any form or by any means - electronic, mechanical, photocopying, recording or otherwise - without the prior written permission of the publisher, except in the case of brief quotations embodied in critical articles or reviews and as permitted under Australian copyright law.

AI-Generated Content Notice. This book includes AI-generated images. While these images were created using artificial intelligence tools, the author has edited, curated and adapted them to fit the vision of this book. Under Australian copyright law, AI-generated works may not be eligible for copyright protection. However, the selection, arrangement and contextual use of these images are considered part of the author's original creative expression and are protected as such.

Disclaimer. This book is intended for informational and personal development purposes only. The author does not provide medical, psychological, legal or financial advice. The interpretations and insights shared are subjective and should not be considered definitive guidance. Always trust your intuition and consult a qualified professional where necessary.

ISBN 978-1-7640433-2-8
First Edition
Printed Worldwide

For more information, visit: thesacredspacepress.com

Cover and interior design by Abigail Henry

To the soul connections that transcend time - the ones who walk beside us in this life and beyond, whispering reminders of who we are and who we have always been.

To the kindred spirits, past and present, who have woven their threads through my journey - friends, teachers, clients and loved ones - thank you for the sacred reflections and the mirrors of truth you have offered.

And to my ancestors, seen and unseen, whose wisdom lives in my bones and whose quiet guidance continues to light the way.

This book is for you - a remembrance, a reconnection, a reverent return to the Eternal Self.

About Me

My journey with divine energy has taken me across continents, but one truth has remained constant: a deep, unwavering love for healing and guiding others home to themselves.

For decades, I have walked alongside seekers as a Reiki Master, Practitioner and Teacher - offering Reiki healing, energy clearing and intuitive Tarot readings for guidance and soulful insight. My passion lies in helping others release emotional blockages, rediscover their light and reconnect with their inner wisdom. It has been my privilege to mentor many beautiful souls on their spiritual paths, supporting them in finding clarity, balance and peace.

My spiritual path is a rich tapestry woven from ancient traditions, soul remembrance and intuitive awakening. It began in Cape Town, South Africa, where I first experienced the transformative power of energy healing and has since unfolded through sacred work across Ireland, the UK, Europe, New Zealand and Australia.

Deeply rooted in ancestral wisdom - my maternal grandmother read tea leaves and my paternal grandfather practised ancient folklore healing - my journey has always been guided by spirit. Their gifts, along with my own intuitive knowing, inspire me to live, teach and write in a way that honours the sacred threads connecting past, present and soul purpose.

My first book, *The Tarot Journey: Affirmations, Mindfulness Colouring and Soul Journaling with the Major Arcana*, was born from this lineage of love and ancestral wisdom. More than just a book, it is an invitation to pause, reflect and connect with the sacred language of the Tarot - using affirmations, creative exploration and intuitive journaling as pathways to inner guidance.

That vision deepened with my second book, *Whispers To My Soul: Awakening the Inner Voice*, which offers fifty-two affirmations and soulful rituals aligned with the chakra system and emotional healing. Through weekly reflections, mindful colouring and gentle practices, it encourages you to honour your energy, trust your rhythm and listen to the quiet wisdom within.

Together with *Sacred Threads: Remembering Past Lives, Soul Connections & the Eternal Self*, these three works form a soul-led trilogy. *The Tarot Journey* opens the path of awakening - introducing the reader to symbolic insight and intuitive connection. *Whispers To My Soul* invites embodiment - grounding spiritual truths into everyday life through ritual and reflection. *Sacred Threads* completes the arc through expansion - exploring the timeless nature of the soul, past life remembrance and the divine threads that weave us across lifetimes.

Each book stands on its own, yet together they offer a layered journey of self-discovery and soul remembrance - from insight to embodiment, from present awareness to eternal knowing.

Wherever you are on your path, I am honoured to walk beside you. May these offerings be companions to your soul - reminding you of your strength, your light and the sacred thread that has always connected you to your truth.

With Love, Light & Laughter

Abigail

The Weaving Pathway

Introduction

The Sacred Thread of Past Lives - A Soul's Journey Across Time - Why We Remember - How This Book Weaves Together - Opening Visualisation: The Loom of Light

Part I: Remembering Past Lives

Chapter 1 - The Eternal Self: I Am Beyond Time
- Mirror Gazing with the Soul - Meeting the Eternal Self - Infinity Mandala *(Timelessness)*

Chapter 2 - Past Life Echoes: The Lives Within You
- Guided Past Life Regression - Listening to Soul Memories - Spiral Mandala *(Cycles of Memory)*

Chapter 3 - Karmic Threads: Healing What Was
- Fire Release Ritual - Untangling Karmic Threads - Celtic Knot Mandala *(Karmic Patterns and Release)*

Part II: Soul Connections

Chapter 4 - Sacred Agreements: Choosing the Path
- Rewriting Your Soul Contract - Honouring Sacred Agreements - Feather & Scroll Mandala *(Sacred Contracts)*

Chapter 5 - Soul Connections: Across Lifetimes
- Calling in Soul Allies - Threads Between Us - Tree of Life Mandala *(Soul Family Roots and Branches)*

Part III: The Eternal Self

Chapter 6 - Soul Gifts: What Your Soul Remembers
- Soul Gift Activation - Awakening Sacred Gifts - Lotus Mandala *(Awakening Ancient Gifts)*

Chapter 7 - Woven Wholeness: Living as the Soul You Are
- The Weaving of Wholeness - Golden Thread Reflections - Weaving Mandala *(Integration and Wholeness)*

Part IV - The Continuing Thread

Chapter 8 - Closing Reflection: Weaving Your Own Sacred Thread
- Integrating Your Sacred Thread - Carrying the Thread Forward - Eternal Weave Mandala *(Your Continuing Journey)*

Thank you

Introduction: The Thread That Remembers

The Sacred Thread of Past Lives

There is a golden thread that moves through you - unseen yet unmistakable. It does not speak loudly, but if you are quiet enough, you can feel its presence in the pauses between breaths and in the places your heart stirs without reason. It shows itself when you walk into a place you have never been and feel like you are returning. It pulses when you meet a stranger who feels like family. It reveals itself in dreams, in symbols, in unexplained fascinations. This is the sacred thread of your soul's memory.

We are not born as blank slates. We do not arrive in this life untouched or untethered. Our souls carry the echoes of lifetimes past - the lessons we have learned, the gifts we have cultivated, the wounds we have yet to heal. These memories may not be consciously accessible, but they are encoded in the fabric of our being. They shape the way we move through the world, the relationships we are drawn to, the talents that come easily and the fears that make no sense in the context of our current experience.

Remembering past lives is not about becoming obsessed with who we were. It is not about reenacting ancient identities or losing ourselves in a search for dramatic stories. It is about returning to what is real and true. It is about integrating the wisdom that our soul already carries and using it to live more consciously in this life.

Often, our soul memories do not come through as movie-like visions. Instead, they come through as quiet knowing's, strong emotional reactions, irrational fears or intense pull toward a particular culture, place or era. A love for a type of music you have never studied. A fear of water despite never having experienced trauma around it. An uncanny ability to understand spiritual concepts you have never been taught. These are the threads - subtle, sacred and significant.

Each lifetime we have lived has left an imprint. Our soul's tapestry is woven from threads of love and loss, power and humility, creativity and silence, trauma and triumph. The remembering is not about retrieving every detail but about understanding the patterns. The threads that show up again and again. The lessons we have returned to master. The stories we are still completing.

And so, we remember - not to dwell in the past, but to live more fully in the present. To bring compassion to our shadows. To embrace our gifts without fear. To honour the soul's long, winding, beautiful journey.

We remember to soften into compassion - for ourselves and others. When we understand that the person we are now is the result of many lifetimes of experience, it becomes easier to forgive ourselves. We begin to see that our challenges are not failures but invitations. Our sensitivities are not weaknesses but soul markers. Our longing for meaning is not restlessness but remembrance.

This sacred thread also runs through our relationships. The people we feel connected to, challenged by or instantly drawn toward are often part of our soul group. We have danced with them before - in other roles, in other stories, across other timelines. Sometimes the connection is loving and supportive. Sometimes it is turbulent and triggering. But always, it is purposeful. These relationships carry karmic threads. Sacred contracts. Opportunities for healing, growth and mutual evolution.

When we allow ourselves to remember, we begin to relate differently. We move from judgment to understanding. From blame to curiosity. From fear to forgiveness. We stop asking, "*Why is this happening to me?*" and start asking, "*What am I being invited to learn, heal or complete?*"

The same remembering applies to our soul purpose. What you feel called to in this life is often an echo of a role you have carried before. A healer who instinctively knows how to work with energy. A teacher who effortlessly inspires. An artist who feels guided by something greater. These are not new roles - they are ancient callings remembered in a new form.

Your soul is not bound by time. It is not limited by form. It has moved through lifetimes of experience and emerged not broken but wise. Not fragmented but evolving. Every thread, even those that feel frayed or unfinished, belongs. Every piece is sacred.

As you begin this journey of *Sacred Threads*, know that you are not beginning from nothing. You are beginning from everything. Your soul already knows the way. It is already holding the thread. And now is the time to follow it.

You are not just a weaver. You are the thread itself - woven through time, love and transformation.

Welcome to your remembering.

A Soul's Journey Across Time

You are not merely a body or a name or a role you play in this life. You are a soul - a luminous, eternal being who has walked through centuries, worn many faces, lived many stories. You have been a daughter and a father, a warrior and a poet, a healer, a wanderer, a mystic, a mother, a monk. Some lives were quiet. Some were wild. Some ended in pain. Others in triumph. All of them belong to you.

The soul's journey is not linear. It does not follow a straight line from point A to point B. Rather, it moves in spirals, sacred loops and luminous weavings. It learns through contrast - joy and sorrow, clarity and confusion, connection and isolation. It grows not by escaping the world but by immersing in it again and again, with increasing awareness, love and truth.

You are the current embodiment of your soul's unfolding. The life you are living now is not random. It is part of a much bigger design - a divine tapestry. Each incarnation you have ever lived contributes a unique colour and texture to that tapestry. Each lifetime adds another thread to your becoming.

Some threads shine with light, reflecting the lives in which you loved deeply, taught others, created beauty or healed pain. Others may feel tangled or dim - remnants of lifetimes where trauma, betrayal or fear left a residue that has not yet fully healed. And yet, every thread has a place. Every story serves a purpose. Nothing is wasted in the soul's journey.

Your past lives do not live behind you. They live within you. And sometimes, they rise to the surface - not as full memories, but as stirrings. That inexplicable pull to a certain culture or era. A fear that does not match anything from this life. A natural gift you have never studied. A longing you cannot name. These are the soul's whispers.

We often think of time as a straight line. But the soul experiences time as layers, loops and echoes. In the quantum field of consciousness, your past, present and future selves coexist, influence each other and offer mirrors for transformation. When you heal something in this life, you may be healing many versions of you at once. When you remember a gift now, you may be reclaiming the power you once set down long ago.

You are not just walking a path - you are weaving one. And every step you take is informed by the lives you have lived before. What you fear, what you crave, what you resist, what you celebrate - it all holds clues. This lifetime is an opportunity to bring together the scattered pieces, to integrate what was and to choose what will be.

The soul does not seek perfection. It seeks growth. Growth in awareness, in compassion, in sovereignty. It returns not to "get it right," but to love more freely, to live more truthfully, to remember more fully. It chooses certain lessons, themes and people not as punishment but as catalysts.

You may have lived lifetimes of service - tending to others, holding sacred space, working with energy or nature. You may have experienced lifetimes of suppression - silenced for your truth, punished for your gifts or misunderstood for your vision. All of that lives in your energetic body now. And all of it wants to be acknowledged, honoured and if needed, healed.

There is power in seeing yourself not just as "someone who is spiritual," but as a soul who has walked the earth many times with sacred intention. This perspective changes everything. It softens judgment. It expands compassion. It deepens humility. It empowers choice.

You stop asking, *"What's wrong with me?"* and begin asking, *"What is this lifetime asking me to remember, embody or complete?"*

This awareness also brings clarity to your relationships. Your soul does not travel alone. You are part of a greater web of souls - a soul group - who incarnate together in different combinations and roles to help each other grow. You may feel this when someone enters your life and instantly feels familiar, even if they challenge you. You are likely journeyed with them before.

Some of these connections feel light and loving. Others stir deep emotions, mirror your shadows or push your limits. But all of them are sacred. All are part of the weaving.

Likewise, your gifts are not new. They are echoes of mastery. You may have been an herbalist, an oracle, a leader, a guardian. The skills you now feel called to develop may be ones you have used before. This lifetime offers you the chance to expand those gifts, to refine them and perhaps to share them in ways you could not before.

And your wounds? They, too, are carried forward. Not as punishment, but as sacred threads in need of light. The fear of being seen, the resistance to speaking your truth, the pattern of self-sacrifice - these may be old stories asking to be rewritten. When you heal them here, you heal them everywhere.

The soul's journey across time is vast, mysterious and beautiful. It cannot be fully grasped by the mind. But it can be felt by the heart. It can be honoured by your willingness to listen, to reflect, to open.

This is not about unlocking every past life detail. It is about noticing what lives in your bones, what flickers behind your eyes, what calls from your dreams. It is about letting your soul lead.

So, take a breath. Feel your feet on the earth. Know that you are the sum of many sacred lives and yet more than the sum. You are a soul in motion. A weaver of light. A thread in the great tapestry of time.

This is your soul's journey across time. And it has brought you here.

Why We Remember

Why do we remember? This question is not simply intellectual - it is spiritual. It arises from the part of us that senses there is more to our existence than what we can touch, explain or recall with the mind. Deep inside, the soul carries memories far older than this lifetime. And it longs to be seen, acknowledged and understood.

We remember not to escape the present or indulge in fantasy, but to retrieve the wholeness that lives within us. Memory, in the soul's language, is a sacred form of returning. When we remember, we reclaim forgotten aspects of ourselves. We uncover soul fragments waiting to be reintegrated. We bring light to patterns, pains and purposes that have travelled with us across lifetimes.

Remembering does not always involve vivid visions or detailed timelines. Often, it is more subtle. It may come as a persistent curiosity, an unexplained fear, a magnetic pull to a culture or tradition or a spontaneous burst of emotion that defies context. These are breadcrumbs from the soul, quietly inviting us to explore what lies beneath.

When we remember, we begin to understand our wounds differently. What once felt random or unfair begins to make sense. A fear of visibility might be traced to a past life where you were punished for speaking your truth. A pattern of abandonment could originate from a lifetime where you lost those you loved. A talent for healing may be a soul gift cultivated over centuries. The remembering gives context. It provides insight. And most importantly, it offers an opportunity for healing.

The soul does not forget. It holds everything - your joy, your grief, your mastery, your heartbreak, your medicine. When we tune in, we begin to hear its whisper. And that whisper becomes a guiding voice.

There is also a sense of sacred timing in remembrance. You remember when you are ready. Not before. Not too late. Always in alignment with your capacity to receive and your willingness to grow. Some memories surface gently, others through dreams, energy work, rituals, synchronicities or soul encounters. However they come, they are sacred.

And while some memories are painful, they do not return to re-traumatise. They return to be healed. What we bury in shadow continues to influence us unconsciously. When brought to light, it loses its grip and becomes wisdom. That is the gift of remembrance: liberation. We remember to release. We remember to forgive. We remember to reclaim.

Forgiveness is one of the deepest medicines remembrance can offer. Forgiveness of self, of others, of the stories we have carried. When we begin to understand the soul's journey - not just in theory, but in felt experience - resentments soften. Judgment fades. Compassion takes root. We begin to view ourselves and others as evolving souls, not broken people.

We also remember so we can live more consciously. When we understand our soul history, we become more intentional in how we walk forward. We become stewards of our energy, more discerning with our time, more present in our choices. Our values shift from survival to service, from performance to purpose.

Soul gifts, too, awaken through remembering. The intuition you have always had, the sacred work you are drawn to, the spiritual traditions that feel like home - these are not new to you. They are familiar because you have been here before. You have practiced. You have devoted. You have prepared. Remembrance activates these threads and brings them into your present awareness with power and clarity.

Remembering also deepens your relationships. You begin to notice patterns - not just within yourself, but in how others show up in your life. The people who stir something in you, for better or worse, may have shared lifetimes with you. Your soul family walks with you again and again. Sometimes as friends, sometimes as challengers. Always as mirrors.

This awareness helps us see relationship dynamics not as failures, but as sacred contracts. It does not excuse harm, but it does offer perspective. We begin to ask deeper questions: *"What are we here to learn?" "What old story are we completing?" "How can I approach this connection with greater consciousness?"*

Even grief is transformed through remembrance. Death is not an end for the soul. It is a doorway. And while we grieve the loss of those we love in this life, our souls often know we will meet again. Recognising this does not take away the pain, but it does offer comfort. It reminds us that connection is never truly lost.

There is also a collective reason for remembrance. As more people awaken to their soul's journey, the frequency of the collective rises. When you remember, heal and embody your light, you ripple that vibration outward. Your personal healing becomes ancestral healing. Your transformation becomes collective medicine. You are not doing this work in isolation. You are part of a greater weaving.

So why do we remember? We remember because we are ready to live as whole souls, not fragmented personalities. We remember because the time of forgetting is ending. We remember because the world needs souls who walk in truth, compassion and power.

And most importantly, we remember because it is who we are.

This book, *Sacred Threads*, is a companion on that journey. It is not a doctrine. It is a mirror. A map. A sacred invitation. Through teachings, reflections, practices, rituals, affirmations and mindful colouring, it will guide you back to yourself. You do not need to understand it all at once. You do not need to force anything. Simply listen. Trust. Follow what stirs. Let your soul lead.

You are already remembering. You are already awakening. You are already holding the thread.

How This Books Weaves Together

This book is not just something to read; it is a journey to be experienced, a tapestry of practices, reflections and creative moments that guide you back to the deepest truth of who you are.

Every page has been created with the intention of helping you remember your Eternal Self, heal old threads, reconnect with soul wisdom and live fully aligned with your soul's truth. Each chapter is a sacred thread and when woven together, they create something far greater than the sum of their parts - a living, breathing soul-weaving journey.

This book invites you to move slowly, intentionally and with an open heart. Each element - Affirmations, Thread Rituals, Soul Spark Reflections, Mindful Colourings and space for journaling - plays a unique role in the weaving and together they create a layered, multi-sensory experience that honours the mind, body and spirit.

The Golden Threads of This Journey
The practices you will find in these pages are not random additions. They are placed intentionally, like carefully chosen threads, to guide you through remembrance, release and integration. Each element has a purpose:

Affirmations - The First Golden Thread
Each chapter begins with an Affirmation Thread and this is intentional. Affirmations are the first golden stitch in the weaving - the moment where you consciously set the energy for the chapter ahead.

An affirmation is more than just a positive statement; it is a soul reminder - a declaration of truth that speaks directly to the deepest part of you. As you read or speak these affirmations, you awaken the memories your soul already holds. You affirm: I remember. I recognise this truth. I honour it in this moment.

Every time you whisper an affirmation, you are weaving that truth into your energy field. You might feel a shift - a lightness, a deep breath or a simple sense of calm knowing. This is how the soul responds to being spoken to in its own language.

The affirmations are intentionally written to align with the energy of each chapter. They are your first invitation to step into that chapter's theme, whether it is healing karmic threads, reconnecting with soul gifts or embracing your wholeness.

Thread Rituals - Living the Wisdom in Your Body
Where affirmations speak to the mind and heart, Thread Rituals invite you to embody the chapter's wisdom. A ritual turns an idea into a lived experience - it allows you to feel the energy shift within you.

Each ritual is simple, sacred and practical. Whether you are mirror gazing to meet your Eternal Self, writing and burning old karmic agreements or visualising yourself weaving your wholeness, these rituals are not just symbolic gestures - they are energetic actions.

Think of them as soul activations. Each ritual gives you the chance to stop reading for a moment and let the teaching move from the page into your body, your breath and your energy field.

You do not need to do them perfectly. Simply approaching them with sincerity and presence allows the threads to move. Many readers describe these moments as the ones where the chapter "comes alive" - where understanding moves from being intellectual to something deeply felt.

Soul Spark Reflections - Listening to Your Own Wisdom
After the ritual, you are invited into Soul Spark Reflections - a space to pause, breathe and listen deeply to yourself. These are not ordinary journaling prompts; they are questions carefully designed to spark remembrance and unlock the wisdom that already lives within you.

Your answers are your soul speaking back to you. Sometimes the responses will surprise you, sometimes they may feel like a whisper of truth you have always known. There is no right or wrong way to reflect; simply let your words flow without judgment.

This reflective process is important because it helps you weave the chapter's teachings into your personal story. The ritual activates energy; the reflection integrates it. By writing (or simply contemplating if you prefer), you are giving your soul a voice.

Over time, you may notice patterns in your reflections - threads of memory, recurring soul lessons or deeper truths rising again and again. These are the golden threads guiding you home to yourself.

Mindful Colouring - Weaving in Stillness
The final element of each chapter is the Mindful Colouring Mandala or Sacred Symbol. This might seem like a creative extra, but it is a powerful tool for integration.

When you colour, you enter a state of quiet focus where the mind softens and the soul can whisper. This simple, meditative action allows everything you have read, felt and reflected on to settle gently into your energy field.

Each mandala or symbol is intentionally chosen to hold the energy of the chapter - the Tree of Life for soul connections, the Lotus for reawakening gifts, the Golden Weaving Mandala for wholeness. As you colour, you are not just creating art; you are weaving your own energy into the chapter's medicine, anchoring the soul lesson in a creative, tactile way.

Many readers keep their finished mandalas as visual reminders of their journey, returning to them as touchstones of what they have healed and remembered.

Sacred Notes - Space to Weave Your Soul Thread
Each chapter closes with space for your reflections - a quiet sanctuary for your own Sacred Notes. These pages are not blank by accident; they are invitations. Here, you are free to capture the whispers, insights, memories and symbols that arise as you journey through these teachings. By writing, sketching or simply letting your thoughts rest upon the page, you begin to weave your soul thread into the tapestry of this work. These notes become a living record of your journey - a bridge between the words you read and the truths you remember.

The Tapestry You Are Weaving
Each chapter is a thread and every time you engage with these practices - speaking the affirmation, embodying the ritual, reflecting on your Soul Sparks and colouring with intention - you are weaving these threads together into your own sacred tapestry.

This book is not meant to be rushed. Move at your own pace. Some chapters may feel light and easy; others may stir deep emotions or memories. Trust that whatever arises is part of your weaving.

Over time, you may notice subtle changes - a softer heart, clearer intuition or a sense of peace even in life's challenges. These are signs that your soul is aligning, that you are remembering who you are and that you are weaving your life consciously, thread by sacred thread.

When you finish this book, your weaving does not stop. In many ways, it is only beginning. The affirmations can be spoken daily. The rituals can be repeated whenever you need to shift energy. The reflections can be returned to again and again as you grow. And the mandalas can continue to remind you of the soul lessons you have embraced.

Every thought, every choice, every loving action is now part of your sacred thread. You are the weaver, the thread and the tapestry all at once.

May this journey remind you that you are eternal, whole and deeply loved. And may the golden threads you weave from this day forward shine brightly - for you and for every soul whose life you touch.

Opening Visualisation

The Loom of Light

Before you step into the sacred work of remembering, take a moment to attune yourself to the soul space in which this journey unfolds. This visualisation - *The Loom of Light* - is a gentle initiation, awakening the threads of your soul memory and connecting you to the timeless self that has always been.

You may read this silently, speak it aloud or record it in your own voice and listen with your eyes closed. Let the words guide you inward.

Begin
Find a quiet space where you will not be disturbed. Sit or lie down in a comfortable position. Close your eyes and take a slow, deep breath in... and out.

Feel your body begin to settle. Allow your shoulders to soften, your jaw to unclench, your belly to expand as you breathe. Let the weight of the day fall away, as if it were sliding off your skin.

Bring your attention to your breath. Inhale gently... and exhale fully. With each breath, imagine yourself sinking deeper into stillness - deeper into presence, deeper into sacred space. With every exhale, release what you no longer need. With every inhale, welcome peace, welcome light.

The Loom Appears
Now, in your mind's eye, imagine yourself standing in a vast and luminous space. There are no walls here, only an open expanse filled with stars - soft, golden points of light stretching out in every direction, as if you are standing in the heart of the universe itself.

In the centre of this space, you see a radiant loom. It glows with gentle, golden light - ancient, sacred and alive. This is the *Loom of Light*, a sacred instrument woven by your soul across time.

As you step closer, notice the threads already stretched across the loom. Some are shimmering with vibrant colours - gold, indigo, rose, emerald - glowing like constellations. Others are faint, delicate or softly tangled. Each thread represents a lifetime, a memory, a soul connection, a gift, a lesson.

Pause for a moment to simply stand before the loom. Feel the hum of energy radiating from it - warm, familiar, loving. You do not need to name or untangle each thread. Simply acknowledge them. Honour them. Every thread, whether bright or dim, is part of your sacred story.

The Weaver Within
As you stand before the loom, you feel a quiet realisation awakening within you - you are not only the witness of this loom; you are the weaver.

See yourself lifting a luminous golden thread between your fingers. This thread represents the life you are living now. Feel its warmth pulsing gently, alive with possibility.

Watch as it weaves itself through the loom - intertwining with threads of the past, threads of future potential, threads of people, purpose and places you are yet to meet. With every movement, light begins to ripple across the loom - soft, warm waves of radiance, wrapping around you like a cocoon of love.

This is the light of remembrance. This is your soul's wisdom reawakening. Feel it moving through you, whispering, *"You have always known the way."*

Activation
Now, speak these words silently or aloud. Let them echo through your heart, through your very being:

"I open myself to the remembering.
I honour every thread I have ever woven.
I call back my soul gifts, my wisdom and my truth.
I trust the path, I trust the process, I trust my Eternal Self.
I am ready to remember. I am ready to heal.
I am ready to weave a new thread of light."

Feel these words resonate through your chest, down your spine, into your bones and outward into your energy field, as if the loom itself is responding to your call.

Return
The loom glows brighter for a moment, as if acknowledging you, before softening into a steady, golden radiance. You know it will always be here, waiting for you to return whenever you choose.

Slowly bring your awareness back to your body. Feel your breath moving in and out. Feel the weight of your fingers, your legs, your feet resting on the ground. Wiggle your toes. Roll your shoulders gently. Stretch if it feels right.

When you are ready, open your eyes.

You have entered sacred space.
You are holding the thread.
Let the remembering begin.

Part I: Remembering Past Lives

Chapter I:
The Eternal Self:
I Am Beyond Time

The Timeless Nature of You

You are far more than the life you are living right now. Beneath the roles you play, the name you were given and the experiences that have shaped you, there is a part of you that has always been - whole, wise and unbroken by time.

This is your Eternal Self - the golden thread of your soul that stretches across lifetimes. It has been with you in every joy, every challenge, every relationship and every lesson you have ever experienced.

Your Eternal Self is the part of you that quietly remembers who you truly are, even when you have forgotten. It whispers through intuition, shows itself in your natural gifts and pulls you toward people and places you recognise even if you cannot explain why.

You are not just this single lifetime. You are a soul that has been weaving wisdom for centuries.

The Golden Thread That Remembers

Imagine your soul as a vast tapestry, woven from hundreds of different threads. Each lifetime adds new colours and textures - some bright and joyful, some darker and filled with lessons, others soft and delicate with love. Through it all runs a single shimmering thread - your Eternal Self.

This thread connects every life you have ever lived. It carries the gifts you have developed, the love you have shared, the wisdom you have earned and even the challenges you have faced and overcome. It never breaks.

You have felt this thread, even if you did not recognise it at the time. You may have stepped into a place you have never been before and felt instantly at home. You may have learned something new and been surprisingly good at it, as though your hands already knew what to do. You may have met someone and felt an instant connection, like greeting an old friend after years apart.

These are not coincidences. These are your soul's memories gently stirring, reminding you that you have been here before.

Why We Forget and Why We Remember

You might wonder, *"If my soul remembers, why don't I? Why don't we arrive in this life with full knowledge of who we have been?"*

The truth is, forgetting is part of the soul's journey. Imagine carrying the weight of every mistake, every loss, every joy from hundreds of lifetimes all at once - it would be overwhelming. We are meant to live fully in the present, to grow and learn through fresh experiences, not to be burdened by every past one.

But the soul never truly forgets. What you need for this lifetime - the wisdom, the talents, the emotional strength - filters through in ways you can use. That's why your intuition feels so trustworthy, why some skills come so easily and why you feel drawn to certain people or places. The memories are not gone; they are simply stored in the deeper layers of your being, rising only when you need them.

The Eternal Self knows when to whisper and when to stay quiet, gently guiding you while allowing you to live freely in this lifetime.

Stories of the Eternal Self

The Eternal Self rarely announces itself in big, dramatic ways. More often, it reveals itself quietly - through instincts, longings and subtle moments that feel so natural we almost overlook them. Yet these are the moments that whisper, *"You have been here before. You already know this."*

Here are three moments from my own life where my Eternal Self reminded me of who I have always been.

The Pull of Distant Lands
For as long as I can remember, I have felt a deep longing to travel - not just to explore, but for something I could not explain. Even as a little girl, I would lie on the grass in our back garden, staring up at aeroplanes carving white lines across the sky. I would wonder where they were going, my heart aching with a strange mix of curiosity and yearning, as if some part of me already knew those faraway places.

Certain landscapes would stir something in me just from looking at photographs - rolling green hills, ancient cobblestone streets, cathedrals and old stone temples. They felt less like places I dreamed of seeing and more like places I remembered.

When I finally began to travel, that feeling only deepened. There were moments when I would step into a place for the first time and feel as though I had come home. I would smile to myself for no reason, walking down unfamiliar streets that somehow felt familiar, as if my soul had walked them before.

That is the way the Eternal Self speaks - through longings that tug at our hearts. Often, the places we feel most drawn to are not random at all; they are soul memories, quietly calling us back.

The Knowing That Came Without Words
I have always been able to sense how people feel, even when they say nothing at all. There have been so many moments when I would look at someone and just know - the sadness behind their smile, the heaviness they carried in their shoulders or the quiet worry they did not speak aloud.

It was not something I ever tried to develop. It simply happened. Even when I was younger, friends would sit beside me and start talking about things they had not told anyone else. More than once, someone said, *"I do not know why I am telling you this, but it feels easier with you."*

At the time, I did not think much of it; it felt natural, almost ordinary. But now I understand - this was my Eternal Self remembering. I believe I have been a listener, a guide or a healer across many lifetimes, learning to read the quiet language of energy and emotion. Some gifts are carried so deeply within us that they simply rise when we need them, as if we have been practising them forever.

The Healing That Came From Somewhere Deeper
I remember one Reiki session that still stays with me. As I worked, I felt an instinctive pull to move my hands in a way I had never been taught. Without thinking, I followed it - tracing soft, weaving patterns over the energy field, almost as if I were stitching something unseen back together.

It was not part of any technique I had learned, yet it felt completely natural, as though my hands already knew what to do. My client later told me, *"Whatever you did then, I felt something shift. It was like a weight lifted."*

This has happened many times since - moments when my hands feel guided by something far older than this lifetime. I believe this is my Eternal Self remembering the healer I have been before. These are not new techniques; they are ancient ones, carried deep within me, waiting for the right moment to return.

The Quiet Pull to Sacred Things
Even as a child, I found myself drawn to quiet, sacred moments without really understanding why. I would light candles just to watch their soft glow, sit silently in nature or trace patterns in the dirt with a stick, as though I were writing something important. It felt comforting, familiar, almost like I was slipping back into an old practice.

Now I see it clearly - those small rituals were my soul's way of remembering. I have likely spent many lifetimes in prayer, meditation or spiritual service and those threads were gently weaving themselves back into this life long before I knew what they meant.

Everyday Whispers of Eternity

The Eternal Self does not always announce itself loudly. More often, it speaks through subtle, very human experiences:
- A place that feels like home, even if you have never been there.
- A talent that comes so naturally it feels like you have practised it for years.
- A connection with someone that feels older than this life.
- A longing that does not make sense but won't leave you.

These are soul memories - small threads of recognition gently woven through your daily life. You are not imagining them. They are reminders of who you truly are.

Living Beyond Time

When you begin to see yourself as eternal, something shifts inside you. Life stops feeling like a series of random events and starts to feel like a larger tapestry.

You begin to trust your instincts because they no longer feel like guesses - they feel like ancient wisdom rising. You stop rushing because your soul has all the time in the world to learn. And you look at others with softer eyes, because you know they too are eternal souls, learning, healing and growing just like you.

Even the smallest choices - a kind word, a moment of patience, an act of creativity - feel more meaningful when you understand they are all part of the larger weaving of your soul.

Your Next Step

Before you continue, take a moment to read and connect with the Affirmation Thread on the next page. Let its words remind you of the timeless part of you that has always been here.

When you feel ready, move to the Thread Ritual - Mirror Gazing with the Soul, where you will meet your Eternal Self in a quiet, reflective way.

Affirmation

I AM ETERNAL,

WHOLE AND BEYOND THE LIMITS OF TIME.

MY SOUL IS ANCIENT AND WISE

AND I TRUST THE TRUTH IT CARRIES.

I HONOUR THE LIGHT I HAVE ALWAYS BEEN

AND THE INFINITE SELF I CONTINUE TO BECOME.

Thread Ritual
Mirror Gazing with the Soul

Purpose
To reconnect with the golden thread of your Eternal Self, allowing the deeper, timeless part of you to rise into awareness.
You may feel warmth, emotion or a quiet sense of recognition. There is no right or wrong way to experience this - simply trust whatever comes.

Prepare Your Space
- Find a quiet, comfortable space where you will not be disturbed.
- Have a mirror large enough to see your face clearly and light a candle or soft light if you wish, letting its gentle glow remind you of the eternal light within.

Ground Yourself
- Sit comfortably with the mirror in front of you. Take a few slow, deep breaths, letting your body relax more with each exhale. Whisper quietly: "*I am here. I am ready to remember who I truly am.*"

The Practice
- Look into your own eyes. Gaze softly, without judgment. You are not looking at your face - you are looking beyond it.
- Hold the gaze, allowing your focus to soften. Imagine you are looking past this lifetime into the soul that has always been here.
- Breathe and notice. Thoughts may come, emotions may rise, or you might simply feel calm. Allow whatever comes to be exactly as it is.
- Welcome your Eternal Self, inwardly whispering: "*I see you. I remember you. I honour all that you are.*"
- Stay as long as feels right. Even a few minutes can feel powerful, but if you are comfortable, sit for 5-10 minutes, letting the connection deepen.

Closing
- When you feel ready, gently close your eyes and place a hand over your heart. Take one final deep breath, as if drawing your Eternal Self closer into your awareness.
- Blow out the candle (if used), thanking yourself for taking this sacred time.

NOTES:

Soul Spark

Meeting the Eternal Self

Take a quiet moment to reflect after your Mirror Gazing with the Soul Ritual. Let your words flow freely, without judgment. This is your sacred space to dream, to declare and to weave with the first whispers that rise from your intentions.

When do I feel most timeless?
(What moments, places or experiences make me feel older than my years or deeply connected to something greater?)

What gifts or strengths feel like they have been with me forever?
(What comes naturally to me, as if I have done it before?)

If my Eternal Self could speak to me now, what would it say?
(Write as if your higher self is talking directly to you.)

What would change if I truly trusted that I am eternal?
(How would I act, speak or live differently?)

When you are finished, place your hand over your heart and repeat the affirmation

I honour all that I have been and all that I am becoming.

Sacred Notes
Space to Weave your Soul Threads

Chapter 2:
Past Live Echoes:
The Lives Within You

Recognising Soul Memory in this Life

Your soul remembers everything. Every love, every loss, every lesson you have ever learned is still woven into you. But those memories do not always rise as clear visions or dramatic flashbacks. Instead, they show up as echoes - soft reminders that feel familiar, instinctive or unexplainable.

A longing for a place you have never visited. A skill that feels natural the very first time you try it. A fear or emotional reaction that seems much bigger than the situation. These are your soul's way of whispering, *"You have been here before."*

The lives you have lived are not gone; they are shaping who you are right now. Your instincts, your gifts, even the people you feel deeply connected to are all influenced by those soul memories gently guiding you.

The Soul's Way of Remembering

The soul does not speak in words or pictures. It speaks in feelings, instincts and recognitions that are so subtle we often overlook them. Recognising these soul whispers begins with noticing the familiar - the moments that seem to belong to a much older story than the life you are living now.

Have you ever:
- Walked into a place for the first time and felt instantly at home?
- Picked up a new skill with surprising ease, as though your hands already knew what to do?
- Felt an emotional pull toward certain cultures, music or ancient symbols?
- Reacted strongly to something with fear, sadness or joy that did not seem to belong to this lifetime?

These are past-life echoes - threads of memory slipping quietly into your everyday life.

Some of the most common ways soul memory shows itself include:

Emotional Resonance
Certain emotions are too deep to belong only to this lifetime. An unexplainable fear of water, an overwhelming love for a specific type of music or a sudden sadness when visiting an old battlefield may all be your soul remembering.

Natural Gifts and Familiar Skills
A skill that comes effortlessly - whether painting, healing or even speaking another language - often carries through lifetimes. Your hands remember what your mind has forgotten.

Physical Memory
The body holds memory too. A tightening in the throat when wearing high collars, dizziness at the sight of blood or a birthmark in a significant place are often past-life imprints carried forward in your physical form.

Dreams and Déjà Vu
The dream state is where the soul speaks most freely. You may dream of places or people that feel vividly real or experience déjà vu, where the past brushes against the present, reminding you that you have walked this path before.

Why These Echoes Matter

The soul does not carry memories forward without purpose. Every echo that rises has meaning.

Some appear as gentle reminders of old gifts, nudging you to use them again. Others surface as old wounds ready for healing. And sometimes they simply arrive to remind you of joy - of love, beauty and the sacred moments you have cherished before.

Noticing these echoes is not about clinging to the past. It is about trusting that the wisdom you carry now has been earned over lifetimes. When you realise this, you stop doubting your instincts. You soften toward your struggles, knowing they may be part of a bigger healing cycle. And you live with a greater sense of purpose, aware that everything you do now adds to the tapestry of your soul.

Stories of Past-Life Echoes

Here are some of the ways past-life echoes have appeared in my own life - simple, personal moments that reminded me that my soul has walked this Earth many times before.

My Mother's Fear of Water
My mother has always had a deep fear of water. She can stand on the shore, but the thought of being in a boat or swimming in the sea fills her with anxiety. There is no event in this life to explain it - she has never had an accident or a bad experience with water.

I have always felt this fear was a past-life echo. Perhaps in another lifetime she experienced something traumatic at sea - a sinking ship, a drowning or losing someone she loved to the water. Her conscious mind does not remember, but her soul does, carrying that old memory forward as a protective instinct.

This is how past-life echoes often show themselves - through emotions that feel too big or too deep to belong only to this lifetime.

Childhood Dreams That Felt Real
As a child, I often had vivid dreams of places I had never been - cobblestone streets, stone walls, markets with bright fabrics and spices. They felt so real that I would wake up convinced I had actually been there.

At the time, they were just dreams. But looking back, I believe they were glimpses of lives I had lived before. Children are often closer to their past-life memories because they have not learned to doubt them yet. Those dreams were simply little threads slipping through the veil while my mind was open enough to notice.

The Pull to Sacred Sites
I have always felt deeply drawn to sacred places - old temples, stone circles and ancient ruins - a pull I believe is born from my deep ancestral roots in ancient lands. My lineage is woven through ancient Ireland and Scotland, where the earth remembers the footsteps of my forebears and the stones whisper with stories older than time. Perhaps it is this blood memory or perhaps the imprint of other lifetimes, that calls me back. Even in photographs, these places stirred something inside me - a quiet stirring of recognition, as though I had walked those paths before.

The first time I stood in an ancient stone circle, I placed my hand on the cool surface and felt a strange wave of recognition - a quiet sense of homecoming. It was not dramatic; it was just a deep, peaceful knowing, as if I had stood there many times before. That is how past-life echoes often feel - like greeting an old friend.

Doodling Symbols I Didn't Understand
As a child, I often doodled spirals, circles and strange knot-like patterns in my notebooks without knowing why. They felt natural, almost comforting to draw.

Years later, when I began learning about sacred symbols, I recognised many of them - Celtic spirals, infinity knots and mandala-like designs. I had been drawing them long before I understood their meaning.

Now, I believe my soul was simply remembering. These symbols were already part of me, carried from lifetimes where they were sacred - perhaps used for meditation, protection or prayer. My hands remembered long before my mind caught up.

Meeting Someone You Feel You Already Know
There was a moment when I met someone for the first time and as soon as our eyes met, I felt an overwhelming sense of familiarity. We spoke as if continuing a conversation we had begun long ago. There was no awkwardness, only recognition. Later, through meditation, I understood that this person had been part of my soul family for many lifetimes - a teacher once, a friend in another life and now a companion on my spiritual journey.

These moments remind us that the soul's connections transcend time.

Listening to Your Soul's Echoes

You do not have to force past-life memories or search for them in deep meditation. They surface naturally when you need them, often in quiet, everyday ways.

Start noticing what feels familiar, what moves you deeply or what you are instinctively good at. Ask yourself: *"Why does this feel like home? Where do I feel I have known this before? What is my body feeling right now - warmth, excitement, peace or even sadness?*

The more you notice, the more these threads begin to weave together. Over time, you begin to trust that these quiet reminders are not random - they are your soul gently guiding you, bringing forward the pieces of wisdom you need now.

You Are the Sum of Many Lifetimes

The echoes you feel are not accidents. They are part of who you are. Every kindness you have given, every skill you have learned, every love you have felt is still within you, shaping the person you are becoming.

You are a soul shaped by many lifetimes, carrying wisdom that never fades. And as you begin to notice these echoes - in your dreams, your instincts, your longings - you begin to remember the truth: *You are eternal. You are woven through time. And your soul has never forgotten who you are.*

Your Next Step

Take a moment to read and connect with the Affirmation Thread. Let its words remind you of the ancient wisdom your soul already carries.

When you feel ready, move to the Thread Ritual - Guided Past Life Regression, where you will gently invite your soul to share the memories it is ready to reveal.

Affirmation

I AM ETERNAL,

WHOLE AND CARRIED BY MANY LIVES.

MY SOUL REMEMBERS WHAT MY HEART STILL FEELS

AND I TRUST THE WHISPERS THAT RISE WITHIN ME.

I HONOUR THE LIVES THAT SHAPED ME

AND THE WISDOM THEY BRING TO THIS MOMENT.

Thread Ritual
Guided Past Life Regression

Purpose
To open a doorway to a lifetime that holds healing or wisdom for you now. Trust that whatever arises - an image, emotion or quiet sense of knowing - is exactly what your soul is ready to share.

Prepare Your Space
- Find a quiet, comfortable place where you will not be disturbed. Dim the lights or light a candle if you wish and keep a journal nearby for afterwards.

Ground Yourself
- Close your eyes and take three slow, deep breaths. Imagine roots growing from your feet or spine deep into the Earth. Feel safe, calm and supported. Say to yourself: *"I am safe. I am ready to remember."*

The Spiral Descent
- Visualise a glowing spiral staircase before you. Step onto it and begin to walk down slowly, counting backwards from ten to one. With each step, feel yourself relaxing deeper into your soul's memory.
- At the bottom, you will see a door or archway with the words: *A Lifetime That Holds a Gift for Me Now.*

Enter the Memory
- Open the door and step through. Allow impressions to arise naturally - images, emotions, body sensations or simply a sense of knowing.
- Ask gently: *"Who am I in this lifetime? What am I learning here?"*
- Trust what comes, even if it feels faint or symbolic.

Receive the Gift
- When you feel ready, ask: *"What wisdom or healing does this lifetime offer me now?"* Let one clear message, symbol or feeling emerge.

Returning
- Thank the memory. Step back through the door and return to the spiral staircase. Walk upwards, counting from one to ten.
- Feel yourself fully present in your body. Open your eyes when ready.

NOTES:

Soul Spark
Listening to Soul Memories

Take a quiet moment to reflect after your Guided Past Life Regression Ritual. Let your words flow freely, without judgment. This is your sacred space to dream, to declare and to weave with the first whispers that rise from your intentions.

When do I feel echoes of another lifetime?
(What moments, places or experiences make me feel older than my years or deeply connected to something greater?)

What gifts or strengths feel like they have been with me forever?
(What comes naturally to me, as if I have done it before?)

If a past-life version of me could speak to me now, what would it say?
(Write as if this past self is speaking directly to you.)

What would change if I trusted the memories my soul reveals?
(How would I act, speak or live differently if I honoured these echoes from my soul?)

When you are finished, place your hand over your heart and repeat the affirmation

The memories I need will gently return to me. I honour what my soul reveals.

Sacred Notes
Space to Weave your Soul Threads

Chapter 3:
Karmic Threads:
Healing What Was

Understanding Karmic Cycles

Every choice we make, every action we take, leaves a thread in the tapestry of our soul. Some threads are light and easy - woven from love, kindness and compassion. Others are heavier - formed from pain, fear or choices that caused harm, whether to ourselves or others. Together, these threads create what we call karma.

Karma is not punishment. It is not some cosmic tally of right and wrong waiting to balance itself out. Instead, it is simply energy seeking completion. Every experience we have had leaves behind a thread of learning and if that learning is unfinished, it weaves itself forward into new lifetimes, asking to be healed or understood.

Think of it this way:
- A loving action creates a thread of ease that flows naturally forward.
- A wound left unresolved creates a knot in the tapestry, pulling at the weave until it is untangled.

Healing karmic cycles is not about being perfect; it is about gently untying the knots - forgiving ourselves, forgiving others and releasing old patterns that no longer serve us.

The Threads That Pull Us Back

Karmic threads often show themselves in very ordinary ways.

You might notice:
- Repeating patterns - the same type of relationship, situation or challenge showing up again and again.
- Strong emotional reactions - feelings that seem too big for the moment, like deep anger, sadness or guilt that does not fully belong to this lifetime.
- Instant connections or aversions - meeting someone and feeling as though you have known (or struggled with) them forever.
- A deep pull to heal or help in a way that feels bigger than this life's experiences.

These are not coincidences. They are soul threads being pulled forward, asking to be seen, understood and finally woven into peace.

Why Karmic Cycles Return

Karma is not here to trap you; it is here to free you. Every karmic thread carries a gift - an invitation to grow, to love differently, to make a new choice.

When a karmic cycle reappears in your life, it is not the universe punishing you; it is your soul calling you back to a lesson that was left unfinished. It is saying, *"Here is another chance. This time, you can choose differently."*

A pattern may repeat many times, sometimes over many lifetimes, until the soul finally learns what it came to learn. When you begin to see these patterns as opportunities rather than burdens, they lose their weight.

Ask yourself: *"What is this experience teaching me right now? How can I respond with love instead of fear this time? What would forgiveness - for myself or others - look like here?"*

Every compassionate choice loosens the knot. Every act of understanding weaves a new thread - lighter, softer, closer to the soul's true nature.

Stories of Karmic Threads

The Same Lesson in Different Disguises
For many years, I found myself in situations where I would take on too much responsibility for others - trying to fix, heal or hold everything together. No matter how much I gave, I would often feel drained, unappreciated or even taken for granted.

It took me a long time to see that this was a repeating karmic thread - a pattern of over-giving likely carried from lifetimes where my role was as a caretaker or healer. In those lives, perhaps I sacrificed too much of myself.

In this lifetime, the lesson was not to stop caring - it was to care differently. To give without losing myself, to recognise that helping someone does not mean carrying their entire journey for them. Each time I chose to step back with love instead of rescuing, I could feel that knot loosening.

A Sudden, Deep Anger That Was Not Mine
There was a time when I reacted strongly to a particular type of authority - not because of anything they did in this life, but because it triggered something much older. The anger felt out of proportion, as if I were remembering a time when power had been misused over me.

Rather than push the anger away, I sat with it, asking quietly, *"Where is this really from? What is it teaching me now?"*

The answer was clear: this lifetime was giving me a chance to find my voice, to stand firm without fear. The karmic thread was not about fighting authority again; it was about healing by responding differently - with calm strength instead of silent resentment.

The Knot Between My Mother and the Water
Even my mother's fear of water feels like a karmic thread - one that may not even be hers alone. Karmic patterns often weave through families or soul groups and I have always felt her fear carried a bigger story.

Watching her avoid water with such instinctive anxiety has reminded me how much of our soul's story lives beneath the surface. Whether she chooses to heal it in this lifetime or not, simply recognising it with compassion feels like a healing thread in itself - breaking cycles of fear by meeting them with understanding instead of judgment.

A Soul Drawn to Healing Work
Many healers feel an unexplainable pull to help others, even when it feels overwhelming. A woman I worked with described feeling an almost desperate need to "save" people. Through meditation, she saw a life where she had been a healer during a plague, unable to save many she loved.

Her soul carried that unfinished grief, pushing her to try again in this life. But this time, her lesson was not to save everyone - it was to learn that offering compassion was enough, even when the outcome was beyond her control.

The Gift Within Karmic Threads

It is easy to see karma as something heavy, but karmic threads are not here to weigh you down. They are here to teach you how to love more deeply, forgive more fully and remember your true nature.

Every knot carries a gift. Sometimes that gift is strength, sometimes compassion, sometimes wisdom. And often, the greatest gift is learning to forgive yourself - for the choices you made when you didn't yet know better.

Karma is not about perfection; it is about evolution. Each lifetime gives you a chance to choose differently, to respond with more love, to weave lighter threads into your soul's tapestry.

Listening for Karmic Echoes

You may wonder how to recognise which patterns in your life are karmic. The answer is simple: they feel persistent. They show up again and again, often in different forms, until you begin to notice them.

Take a quiet moment to ask yourself: *"Where in my life do I feel stuck in the same cycle? Which emotions feel older than this lifetime? Who in my life feels like a soul I have known before?"*

When you feel these threads pulling at you, pause. Instead of reacting automatically, breathe and ask: *"What is the highest way I can respond this time?"* Even a small act of kindness or forgiveness can shift the energy of a karmic thread.

Healing Karmic Threads in This Lifetime

You do not need to know every past-life detail to heal karmic patterns. Often, the healing happens simply by choosing differently in the present.

Some gentle ways to begin untangling karmic knots include:

- Awareness - noticing when the same pattern repeats and asking what it is teaching you.
- Forgiveness - not for others' sake, but to free your own heart.
- Self-compassion - releasing guilt for past mistakes, knowing every lifetime is part of learning.
- Acting with love now - each time you choose love over fear; you weave a new thread.

Karmic healing is not instant. But each small, conscious choice creates ripples, softening old knots and allowing your soul to feel lighter.

You Are Not Your Past

The most important thing to remember is this: You are not bound by your past

Your soul may carry these threads forward, but you are not trapped by them. Every time you make a conscious, loving choice, you change the pattern. Every time you offer yourself compassion, you untangle another knot.

You are not being judged. You are not being punished. You are simply learning. And with each new choice, you are weaving a future that is lighter, freer and more aligned with your soul's truth.

The Thread of Healing

Imagine every karmic knot you untie as a thread turning golden, weaving itself back into your soul's tapestry with peace. Every time you choose kindness, forgiveness or a new way of responding, you change not just this lifetime, but the energy of the lifetimes before it.

Healing karma is not about erasing the past. It is about honouring it, learning from it and weaving it into something more whole.

Your Next Step

Take a moment to read and connect with the Affirmation Thread. Let its words remind you that you are no longer bound by old knots - you are free to weave something new.

When you feel ready, continue with the Thread Ritual - Fire Release Ritual, where you will gently release what no longer serves you and honour the threads you are ready to let go.

Affirmation

I AM ETERNAL,

WHOLE AND LEARNING THROUGH TIME.

MY SOUL UNDERSTANDS THE PATTERNS I HAVE WALKED

AND I TRUST THE WISDOM THEY BRING.

I RELEASE WHAT NO LONGER SERVES ME

AND I HONOUR THE HEALING UNFOLDING THROUGH TIME.

Thread Ritual
Fire Release

Purpose
To release old karmic energy, patterns or emotional loops that no longer serve your soul's growth, allowing space for new, lighter threads to weave into your life.

Prepare Your Space
- Choose a quiet space where you feel safe and undisturbed.
- You will need: A small fireproof bowl, candle or fireplace; paper and a pen and a heatproof dish or sand to extinguish the flame

Ground Yourself
- Sit comfortably and take three slow, deep breaths. Visualise roots growing from your feet or spine deep into the Earth, anchoring you in safety and strength.
- Whisper softly: *"I am safe. I am ready to release what no longer serves me."*

Write the Threads
- On a piece of paper, write down anything you feel ready to release - Examples include: Repeating patterns, emotional pain, old beliefs, karmic relationships.
- You can write a single word, a list or even a letter to your past self.

The Fire Offering
- On a piece of paper, write down anything you feel ready to release. Examples include: Repeating patterns or old emotional wounds, limiting beliefs or fears, karmic relationships or attachments.
- You can write a single word, a list or even a letter to your past self. Trust whatever rises first.

The Fire Offering
- Hold the paper in your hands and whisper: *"I thank you for all you have taught me. I no longer need to carry you. I release you now with love."*
- Light the paper carefully and place it in the fireproof bowl.
- As it burns, imagine golden threads gently unravelling and dissolving into light, freeing you from the old energy.

Affirm the Release
- Place your hands over your heart. Take three deep breaths and imagine yourself glowing, lighter and free.
- Say aloud: *I release the past with love. I am free to weave new patterns of peace and wisdom.*

Closing
Allow the ashes to cool, then return them to the Earth or scatter them in flowing water if possible, symbolising the final release.

NOTES:

Soul Spark
Untangling Karmic Threads

Take a quiet moment to reflect after your Fire Release Ritual. Let your words flow freely, without judgment. This is your sacred space to dream, to declare and to weave with the first whispers that rise from your intentions.

What pattern keeps repeating in my life?
(Where do I feel caught in the same loop, no matter how much I try to change it?)

What has this pattern taught me so far?
(What wisdom, strength or understanding has grown because of this experience?)

If I truly forgave myself and others, how would I feel?
(Describe the lightness, freedom or peace that might come.)

What would change if I chose differently next time?
(What new action or response could shift this energy for good?)

When you are finished, place your hand over your heart and repeat the affirmation

I release the past with love. I am free to weave new patterns of peace and wisdom.

Sacred Notes
Space to Weave your Soul Threads

Part II: Soul Connections

Chapter 4:
Sacred Agreements:
Choosing the Path

The Threads We Chose Before We Came Here

Long before you took your first breath in this lifetime, your soul made choices. It chose experiences, lessons and connections that would help you grow. These are known as sacred agreements or soul contracts - the threads you wove with others before arriving here.

Not every agreement is meant to be easy. Some are made with souls who love us so deeply that they agree to play difficult roles so we can grow. Some are joyous bonds with family or friends who travel with us lifetime after lifetime. Others are fleeting but impactful, designed to redirect us, open our hearts or remind us of who we truly are.

Understanding these agreements does not mean excusing hurtful behaviour or staying in unhealthy situations. It simply offers a new perspective: nothing is random. Every soul you meet plays a part in the great weaving of your journey.

Why We Make Soul Agreements

Soul contracts are made from a place of love - even the challenging ones. Before we incarnate, our souls choose experiences that will help us evolve. We come together with other souls, deciding who will help us grow, who will remind us of love and even who will challenge us to stand in our truth.

We make these agreements to:
- Learn specific lessons - such as forgiveness, courage or self-worth.
- Balance karmic threads - healing old patterns or roles from other lifetimes.
- Support each other's growth - agreeing to help another soul reach a breakthrough.
- Share joy and love - sometimes just to experience happiness together again.

You might not consciously remember making these agreements, but your soul recognises them instantly. This is why you feel a strong pull toward certain people or situations - they are part of the path you chose before birth.

Recognising Sacred Agreements in Your Life

You may already sense which relationships carry a deeper soul connection. Here are some signs:
- Instant familiarity - feeling as though you've known someone forever.
- Strong emotional reactions - love, trust, irritation or even conflict that feels much bigger than the present moment.
- Repeating themes - encountering similar lessons with different people until you learn what your soul is asking of you.
- A sense of purpose - feeling guided to help someone or being helped in a way that changes you profoundly.

Not all sacred agreements are lifelong. Some souls enter only for a short time, fulfilling their role before moving on. Every connection, no matter how brief, is part of the greater weaving of your soul's story.

The Power of Choice in Sacred Agreements

Although soul contracts are chosen before birth, you are never bound to them in a way that removes your free will. These agreements are not rigid; their purpose is growth. You always have the power to choose how you respond.

Sometimes an agreement has served its purpose and it is time to release it. Sometimes a connection shifts as both souls evolve. By becoming aware of these agreements, you can consciously decide whether to continue, change or lovingly let them go.

A sacred agreement fulfilled does not always mean a relationship must end - it simply means it can evolve into something lighter, freer and more aligned with who you are now.

Stories of Sacred Agreements

A Friend Who Felt Like Family
Years ago, I met someone who felt like family from the first conversation. We laughed as if we had known each other forever, finishing each other's sentences. There was no awkwardness, only the comfort of recognition.

Over time, I realised this was not just an ordinary friendship - it was a soul agreement. We supported each other through significant life changes, almost as if we had promised to be there for one another.

When our paths eventually shifted apart, there was no sadness, only gratitude. Our agreement had served its purpose - to remind us of unconditional support.

The Teacher Disguised as Challenge
Not all agreements feel loving at first. There was someone in my life who challenged me deeply. Their words often triggered me, stirring old wounds of self-doubt. For a long time, I resisted, wondering why this person was in my life at all.

But when I looked deeper, I realised this was a soul contract designed to teach me boundaries and self-worth. They were not here to hurt me; they were here to hold up a mirror, pushing me to stand firmly in my truth.

Once I learned the lesson, the dynamic shifted. The tension dissolved and I felt free - not because they changed, but because I had.

Family Threads That Run Deep
Family often carries the strongest soul agreements. With some family members, I have felt incredible love and support; with others, there have been misunderstandings and differences that felt heavy.

I have come to see even the difficult dynamics as chosen - opportunities for compassion, forgiveness, or learning patience. Seeing them as sacred agreements has softened my heart, allowing me to meet those relationships with more understanding rather than resentment.

The Stranger Who Changed Everything
Once, a stranger offered me a kindness that shifted the course of my life - a conversation that lasted only a few minutes but gave me the courage to take a leap I had been resisting.

That moment felt too perfectly timed to be chance. I believe it was a sacred agreement - a soul choosing to step briefly into my story to offer exactly what I needed before continuing on their own path. Some threads are short but brilliant, like sparks that ignite change.

The Mentor I Never Met Again
Many years ago, I attended a single workshop taught by a woman I never saw again. Yet her words planted a seed that changed my entire spiritual path.

Sometimes a soul agreement is this simple - two lives brushing briefly, transferring exactly what is needed before moving on. These small encounters can change the course of a lifetime.

Honouring and Rewriting Agreements

Not every agreement is meant to last forever in the same form. Sometimes the lesson has been learned and the agreement can be released or rewritten.

You can honour these connections by:
- Offering gratitude for the lessons learned, even in difficult situations.
- Releasing with love - freeing both yourself and the other soul from old patterns.
- Setting new intentions - choosing to continue the connection in a healthier, lighter way.

When you consciously shift these agreements, you weave new energy into your soul's tapestry - golden threads of peace and love that ripple through lifetimes.

Walking Forward with Love

Every soul you meet is part of your sacred weaving. Some walk with you for a lifetime; others appear only briefly, leaving just a few delicate threads. Yet each plays a role in shaping who you are.

When you see these connections as agreements chosen with love, even the difficult ones begin to make sense. Those who challenge you are mirrors guiding healing; those who bring joy are reminders of love promised long ago.

You are not a victim of chance - you are a soul who chose to grow, to love and to heal through every connection. Walking forward with love means honouring each thread, knowing it is part of a greater design and allowing gratitude to weave more light into your life's tapestry.

The Golden Threads of Choice

Imagine each sacred agreement as a thread of light. Some threads shimmer with joy, some are knotted with lessons, but all are woven into the same tapestry.

With every conscious choice, you can change the weave - softening old knots, adding new colours and turning even the heaviest threads to gold.

You are not just walking through life; you are shaping it. You are not just meeting souls by chance; you are remembering the promises you made to each other before you arrived.

Your Next Step

Take a moment to read and connect with the Affirmation Thread. Let its words remind you that you are free to weave new agreements that serve your highest good.

When you feel ready, move to the Thread Ritual - Rewriting Your Soul Contract, where you will consciously honour these sacred connections and gently release what no longer serves.

Affirmation

I AM ETERNAL,

WHOLE AND GUIDED BY SACRED CHOICE.

MY SOUL REMEMBERS THE PROMISES I MADE BEFORE I CAME.

I TRUST THE LESSONS WRITTEN IN MY PATH.

I HONOUR THE AGREEMENTS THAT SHAPE MY GROWTH

AND I WALK THEM WITH GRACE AND LOVE.

Thread Ritual
Rewriting your Soul Contract

Purpose
To consciously shift or rewrite an old soul agreement, bringing it into harmony with your current growth and highest good.

Prepare Your Space
- Find a quiet place where you feel safe and centred.
- Light a candle or hold a crystal that feels calming or protective.
- Have paper and a pen ready.

Ground Yourself
- Sit comfortably, close your eyes and take three slow breaths.
- Visualise roots growing from your feet deep into the earth, anchoring you.
- Say quietly: *"I am safe. I am ready to rewrite what no longer serves my soul."*

Call in the Soul Agreement
- Think of the person or situation you wish to shift.
- Visualise a glowing thread connecting you both.
- Whisper to yourself: *"I honour the agreement we made. I thank you for playing your role in my growth."*

Rewrite the Contract
- On your paper, write a new statement for this connection - Examples include: I now release this karmic pattern and replace it with peace, I choose love, forgiveness and freedom for both of us.
- Be clear and compassionate - imagine what you want this energy to become.

Seal the New Agreement
- Hold the paper to your heart and say: *"This is my new agreement, written in love and light. May it serve the highest good for all involved."*
- Burn the paper safely (or tear it into small pieces), imagining the old energy dissolving and the new one weaving in golden light.

Returning to the Present
- Take a deep breath and visualise the thread between you and the other soul glowing brighter or gently dissolving if it is complete.
- Say aloud: *"I trust the sacred path I have chosen. I walk forward free and guided by love."*

NOTES:

Soul Spark

Honouring Sacred Agreements

Take a quiet moment to reflect after your Rewriting your Soul Contract Ritual. Let your words flow freely, without judgment. This is your sacred space to dream, to declare, and to weave with the first whispers that rise from your intentions.

Who in my life feels like part of a sacred agreement?
(Who has shaped my growth the most, whether through love, support or challenge?)

What lesson might this connection be teaching me?
(What qualities - compassion, forgiveness, strength - am I being called to embody?)

If I could speak to this soul on a higher level, what would I say?
(Write as if you are talking directly to their soul, thanking them for their role.)

What would change if I fully trusted the agreements I made before this life?
(How would I act, speak or live differently if I believed every connection had a purpose?)

When you are finished, place your hand over your heart and repeat the affirmation

I walk the path I once chose with grace. I honour the sacred agreements that guide my soul's growth.

Sacred Notes

Space to Weave your Soul Threads

Chapter 5:
Soul Connections:
Across Lifetimes

The Threads That Bind Us Across Time

Some souls walk with us lifetime after lifetime. They are the ones who feel familiar from the very first moment we meet - the friends we trust instantly, the partners who awaken something deep within us, or even the people who challenge us in ways that feel uncomfortably personal.

These connections are not accidents. They are threads woven long ago, carried through lifetimes as part of our soul's greater story. Some are bonds of love, some are agreements for growth and some are karmic mirrors, reflecting lessons we still need to learn.

Recognising these connections helps us honour them for what they truly are - sacred threads of soul weaving, not random encounters.

Soul Families - Travelling Together Through Lifetimes

Your soul family is a group of souls you travel with across many lifetimes. They may appear in different roles each time - a parent in one life, a sibling or best friend in another, even a fleeting stranger who helps you at a key moment.

Soul families carry a shared purpose: to help each other grow, heal and remember who they truly are. The love within these groups is unconditional, even when the lessons are difficult.

Sometimes your closest soul family members are not the ones who feel the easiest to love. They may push your buttons, hold you accountable, or challenge you to grow. But beneath it all, there is a bond of deep, unwavering love.

The Deep Desire to Be a Mother
For as long as I can remember, I have felt a deep pull to be a mother. Even before I had children of my own, I carried this quiet, unshakable longing - not just for the idea of a family, but for the experience of nurturing, loving and guiding a soul as it grows.

It was as if my children were already calling to me, their souls reaching out long before we ever met in this life. I would sometimes feel their presence in quiet moments - a warmth in my heart, a soft knowing that they were out there, waiting.

It did not feel like hope or wishful thinking; it felt certain, like an invisible thread already connected us.

I believe this is how the Eternal Self speaks - through the strongest desires of the heart. Perhaps I have been a mother in many lifetimes, my soul carrying forward the memory of that love. Some threads are too precious to leave behind and the bond between mother and child is one of the most powerful of all.

The Sibling Who Always Feels Like Home
One of my closest relationships is with a sibling who feels like home in every way. We do not always agree, we sometimes clash, but beneath every disagreement there is an unshakable bond - a love that feels ancient.

I have no doubt we have walked together through many lives, switching roles as needed - parent and child, teacher and student, friend and guide. In this lifetime, we simply chose to return as siblings again, continuing the same thread of love in a different form.

Twin Flames - The Mirror of the Soul

Among the most intense connections you may experience is the twin flame - a soul so deeply linked to yours that they mirror your highest potential and your deepest wounds.

Twin flames are not always romantic partners. Sometimes they are friends, mentors or even brief encounters that shake your life awake.

The twin flame connection can be challenging because it reflects back the parts of yourself you most need to heal. It is not always meant to last forever in a physical sense - its purpose is growth, awakening and alignment with your true self.

The Mirror That Reflected What I Needed to Heal
When I met my husband, I felt a connection that was both magnetic and unsettling - as if I had known him across lifetimes. His presence stirred emotions I could not always name. At times, he reflected back my deepest insecurities, showing me the places where I doubted my own worth. And yet, in the same breath, he inspired me to rise into my truth, to own my voice and to step more fully into who I am.

Like many twin flame connections, it was not always comfortable. He was a mirror to my soul, revealing what I had tried to hide even from myself. In the beginning, I resisted the intensity of that reflection. But over time, I came to see that it was never here to break me - it was here to help me heal.

Through love, patience and the fire of honesty, we continue to grow together. The raw edges softened and what remained was a deep gratitude for the way he had walked beside me, challenging me and loving me in equal measure. In his eyes, I continue to see both the woman I am and the woman I am becoming.

The Friend Who Pushed Me to Shine
A dear friend once challenged me in ways I did not always appreciate. She refused to let me play small, constantly encouraging me to share my work, my voice and my truth with the world.

Looking back, I see she was a twin flame-like mirror, reflecting my own hidden potential and pushing me to step into it. The connection was sometimes fiery, but the love beneath it was undeniable - a soul agreement to help each other grow brighter.

Karmic Mirrors – Lessons Wrapped in Challenge

Not every strong connection is a soul family bond or a twin flame. Some are karmic mirrors - people who arrive to help you untangle old knots.

These relationships can feel heavy or repetitive. You might find yourself drawn to the same type of person again and again or stuck in similar patterns that leave you frustrated.

Karmic mirrors are not here to punish you; they are here to help you recognise and heal old wounds. Once the lesson is learned, the pattern dissolves and the connection often shifts or fades.

The Repeating Pattern
For years, I found myself in friendships where I over-gave, trying to rescue or fix others. Each time I ended up feeling drained and unappreciated.

Eventually, I recognised the pattern for what it was - a karmic thread asking to be healed. In past lives, I may have been a healer or caretaker who sacrificed too much of myself. This lifetime was giving me the chance to choose differently - to help with love but also honour my own boundaries.

The moment I started responding differently, the pattern loosened. Those draining connections gently fell away, making space for healthier, balanced relationships.

The Love-Hate Connection
There was someone in my life who seemed to both frustrate and fascinate me. Our conversations were intense, sometimes argumentative, but I could not deny the magnetic pull.

Through meditation, I saw flashes of a life where we had been rivals - two stubborn souls who never resolved their conflict. This lifetime gave us another chance, not to repeat the rivalry but to finally find respect for each other. Once I saw it that way, the tension eased, replaced with mutual kindness.

Honouring the Souls Who Walk With You

Whether it is a joyful soul family bond, a twin flame mirror or a karmic connection, each soul you meet plays a role in your growth.

You can honour these connections by:
- Recognising them for what they are - chosen agreements, not coincidences.
- Offering gratitude - even for the difficult ones, as they teach the deepest lessons.
- Releasing with love - letting go when a connection has served its purpose.
- Calling in support - consciously inviting soul allies who nurture and uplift you.

Every relationship, whether brief or lifelong, is a thread in your soul's tapestry - part of the weaving that helps you become who you are meant to be.

The Love That Carries Across Lifetimes

The most comforting truth about soul connections is that they never truly end. Even if a relationship changes, even if someone leaves this lifetime, the love you share remains woven into your soul.

Soul family bonds endure. Twin flames continue to mirror you in other ways. Karmic lessons, once learned, transform into lighter, golden threads that carry forward.

You are never alone on this journey. Your soul is always surrounded by allies, teachers and companions - some in this lifetime, others watching over you from beyond.

The Golden Weaving of Love

Imagine every soul connection as a thread of light, woven through time. Some threads are bright with joy, some are knotted with lessons but all are bound by love.

Every time you forgive, honour or release a connection with love, that thread turns golden - shimmering across lifetimes, carrying the memory of healing forward.

You are never just meeting people by chance; you are recognising them. You are remembering the promises you made to walk together, learn together and love each other home.

Your Next Step

Take a moment to read and connect with the Affirmation Thread. Let it remind you of the love and support that surrounds you, both seen and unseen.

When you feel ready, continue with the Thread Ritual - Calling in Soul Allies, where you will consciously invite supportive soul family members and kindred spirits into your life.

Affirmation

I AM ETERNAL,

WHOLE AND DEEPLY CONNECTED THROUGH ALL TIME.

MY SOUL REMEMBERS THOSE WHO WALK BESIDE ME.

I TRUST THE BONDS WE HAVE SHARED BEFORE AND NOW.

I HONOUR THE LOVE AND LESSONS OF THESE CONNECTIONS

AND THE SACRED MIRRORS THEY HOLD FOR ME.

Thread Ritual
Calling in Soul Allies

Purpose
To invite supportive soul family members, guides and kindred spirits - both seen and unseen - into your life, strengthening the connections that nurture your soul's growth.

Prepare Your Space
- Choose a quiet place where you feel calm and grounded.
- Light a candle or place a crystal nearby.
- Have a notebook ready to write any insights that arise.

Ground and Centre
- Close your eyes and take three slow, deep breaths.
- Visualise golden roots growing from your feet deep into the earth, anchoring you in safety and love.
- Whisper to yourself: "*I am safe. I am ready to call in the souls who walk this path with me.*"

Weave the Golden Threads
- Visualise yourself standing in a vast starry space, holding a glowing golden thread in your hands.
- Say softly: "*I now call forth the souls who are part of my sacred family, those who support my highest growth and deepest healing.*"
- Imagine the golden thread extending outward, weaving across time and space, connecting to other glowing threads - each belonging to a soul ally who loves and supports you.

Invite Them In
- See the faces of these soul allies appearing in the golden light. Some you may recognise as people in your current life; others may feel like ancient, unseen guides.
- Whisper: "*Thank you for walking with me. May our connection strengthen for the highest good of all.*"

If you are seeking new soul allies in this lifetime, imagine doors opening, opportunities appearing and kindred spirits being gently drawn into your life.

Seal the Connection
- Place your hands over your heart and say: "*I am open to the love, guidance and support of my soul family. I trust the sacred weaving of these connections.*"
- Feel warmth in your heart as the golden threads glow brighter, sealing this intention.

Returning and Reflect
- Slowly bring your awareness back to your body.
- Open your eyes and write down any names, feelings or messages that came to you during this ritual.
- End by repeating the affirmation: "*I honour the souls who walk beside me. I trust the sacred weaving of love, lessons and growth that guides my path.*"

NOTES:

Soul Spark

Threads Between Us

Take a quiet moment to reflect after your Calling in Soul Allies Ritual. Let your words flow freely, without judgment. This is your sacred space to dream, to declare and to weave with the first whispers that rise from your intentions.

Who in my life feels like part of my soul family?
(Who makes me feel seen, supported and loved for who I truly am?)

Who might be acting as a karmic mirror for me right now?
(What patterns or emotions are they triggering that I am ready to heal?)

What lesson has a challenging soul relationship taught me?
(How has this connection pushed me to grow stronger, wiser or more compassionate?)

How would I act differently if I trusted every soul is here for a reason?
(What would change in how I speak, feel, or respond if I believed every connection has a sacred purpose?)

When you are finished, place your hand over your heart and repeat the affirmation

I honour the souls who walk beside me. I trust the sacred weaving of love, lessons and growth that guides my path.

Sacred Notes
Space to Weave your Soul Threads

Part III: The Eternal Self

Chapter 6:
Soul Gifts:
What Your Soul
Remembers

The Gifts Carried Through Time

There are parts of you that feel older than this lifetime - skills, instincts and talents that seem to come from nowhere, yet feel as natural as breathing. These are your soul gifts, the wisdom you have carried through lifetimes, woven into the eternal fabric of who you are.

Some of these gifts are obvious - you may instinctively know how to heal, to guide or to create beauty. Others lie dormant, waiting for the right time to awaken. The strongest clue that a soul gift is calling to you is the deep sense of familiarity - as though you are not learning something new but remembering what you have always known.

Why Soul Gifts Are Remembered

Soul gifts are never lost. Even if you have lifetimes where they are unused, the wisdom is stored in your soul's memory, ready to reawaken when it can serve your highest good.

You may feel them stirring as:
- A natural talent that develops quickly and effortlessly - something you pick up as though your hands already remember.
- A sudden fascination with a subject you have never studied before - an unexplainable pull toward ancient practices, creative arts or healing work.
- Strong intuitive abilities - flashes of insight or inner knowing, even without formal training.
- A deep calling to help, create or guide others - an urge you cannot logically explain, as if something greater is moving through you.

These gifts are part of your purpose. They are threads your soul has chosen to carry forward, not only for your own growth but to help others in their journeys too.

The Quiet Ways Soul Gifts Show Themselves

Not all gifts are dramatic or obvious. Some are subtle - a calming presence that soothes people, an ability to sense truth beneath words, or a way of inspiring others through kindness and encouragement.

What matters is not how "big" these gifts seem, but how they are used. Every gift, no matter how simple, weaves light into the world when expressed with love.

Remembering the Gifts Within

You do not need to force your gifts to awaken. They re-emerge naturally when you follow your deepest joys, curiosities and callings. Often, they show up long before you consciously recognise them.

The Healing That Came Naturally
Long before I trained formally in Reiki or other energy practices, I instinctively placed my hands on people who were upset or unwell. I didn't know why - I simply felt pulled to do it. My hands would grow warm and often they would say they felt calmer or lighter afterward.

When I eventually learned Reiki, it felt like coming home. Every technique, every principle felt familiar, as though I had practised it many times before. Even now, I often find myself incorporating movements or methods I was never taught - they just come, flowing instinctively from a deeper place.

I believe this is the memory of past-life healing rising through me, woven into my soul long before this lifetime.

The Pull of Sacred Work
There are times when a gift begins to call you before you fully understand it. For me, that call came through my writing. Long before I thought of myself as an author, words, insights and book layouts would arrive in the quiet hours - sometimes in dreams and visions, sometimes in those still moments when the world seemed to fade away. They felt familiar, as though I was remembering them rather than creating them.

Although I did not write much as a child, I felt an unshakable connection to the act of sharing wisdom. Looking back, I believe that in other lifetimes I may have passed on knowledge and healing practices - perhaps through sacred texts, teachings or spoken word. Now, that same calling moves through me in the form of my books, each one a vessel for the practices, rituals and soul teachings my heart knows by memory.

Soul gifts often whisper like this - in instincts, dreams or moments of joy that feel oddly significant.

The Call to Create
For some, soul gifts express themselves through creativity. Perhaps you have felt this too - painting, writing or crafting something that seems to flow through you rather than from you. There are moments when inspiration strikes so deeply it feels as though you are a channel for something greater, as though your soul is simply remembering how to create.

Artists, musicians and creators often describe this feeling - the sense that the work is not entirely theirs, that they are guided by something beyond themselves. This is how soul gifts speak when they move freely: effortless, inspired and deeply fulfilling.

Why Some Gifts Stay Dormant

Not all gifts awaken immediately and there is wisdom in that. Some are meant for later stages of life, when you are ready to hold them with integrity and purpose. Others remain quiet if they are not needed in this lifetime, or if expressing them would distract you from the lessons you are here to learn now.

Trust the timing. Your soul knows when to bring these gifts forward. Some threads are meant to weave quietly in the background, preparing for future lives where they will be needed.

The Gift That Waited for the Right Time
I once knew someone who always felt a quiet fascination with herbal medicine but never pursued it seriously. Then, later in life, she suddenly felt compelled to study it, quickly becoming skilled and intuitive in her practice.

She often said it felt as though she was "picking up where she left off." The timing had simply ripened - her soul waited until the right moment, when she was ready to use the gift for the highest good.

The Unspoken Gifts
Not every gift is meant to be shared in obvious ways. I once met a man whose greatest gift was simply his presence. He was calm, patient and deeply kind; and people naturally opened up around him, feeling safe in his quiet company.

He did not see this as a gift, but it was - his energy shifted people in subtle ways. Many soul gifts work like this, weaving love and healing into the world without grand gestures.

The Golden Thread of Remembering

Every time you use a soul gift, you are not just helping others - you are healing parts of yourself too. These gifts connect you back to lifetimes where you learned them, weaving your past and present into a golden thread of remembrance.

The more you honour these gifts, the stronger the connection becomes and the more naturally they flow. Even when you do not consciously remember where they came from, your soul knows - and it rejoices each time you allow them to shine.

Welcoming Your Soul Gifts Now

Your soul gifts are not meant to remain hidden forever. They are waiting to be expressed, whether in small everyday ways or through deeper soul work.

You can gently invite your soul gifts to reawaken by:
- Following what excites or inspires you, even if it makes no sense.
- Spending time in stillness, asking your higher self to show you what you are ready to remember.
- Allowing creativity, healing or intuition to flow naturally, without self-judgment.
- Trusting that what feels natural to you is often your soul's oldest wisdom.

The gifts you carry are not just for you. They are threads of love, healing and wisdom meant to be shared, whether in quiet everyday ways or through larger soul work.

The Soul's Legacy of Light

Imagine every gift you share as a luminous thread weaving through time. Some were first learned lifetimes ago, some refined through trial and love, all carried forward in the tapestry of your soul.

Each time you use a gift - whether through art, kindness, healing or even a simple smile - that thread glows brighter, linking you to the wisdom of who you have always been.

You are not creating these gifts from nothing; you are remembering. You are reawakening the soul's legacy of light, carried lovingly across time.

Your Next Step

Take a moment to read and connect with the Affirmation Thread. Let it remind you that the wisdom you seek is already within you, waiting to be remembered.

When you are ready, continue with the Thread Ritual - Soul Gift Activation, where you will gently call these gifts forward, inviting them to awaken in love and for the highest good.

Affirmation

I AM ETERNAL,

WHOLE AND GIFTED ACROSS LIFETIMES.

MY SOUL REMEMBERS THE TALENTS I HAVE

CARRIED THROUGH TIME.

I TRUST THE WISDOM AWAKENING WITHIN ME NOW.

I HONOUR THE GIFTS I RECLAIM

AND SHARE THEM AS THE SOUL I AM.

Thread Ritual
Soul Gift Activation

Purpose
To gently awaken and strengthen the ancient talents and wisdom your soul has carried through lifetimes.

Prepare Your Space
- Sit in a quiet, comfortable place where you feel safe.
- Light a candle or place a crystal such as labradorite, amethyst or citrine nearby to amplify your intention.
- Have your journal ready to record any insights.

Ground Yourself
- Close your eyes and take three deep breaths.
- Visualise golden roots anchoring you deep into the earth.
- Say quietly: *"I am safe and ready to awaken the gifts my soul has carried through time."*

Call Forth Your Ancient Gifts
- Place your hands on your heart and imagine golden light glowing within.
- Whisper: *"Show me the gifts I am ready to remember. Awaken what will serve my highest good and the good of all."*
- Sit in stillness, allowing images, feelings or memories to rise. You may sense hands creating, hear a melody, feel healing energy in your palms or simply feel a deep knowing.

Activate Through Intention
- Visualise this golden light spreading through your body, flowing down your arms and into your hands.
- Say: *"I activate the gifts my soul has carried through lifetimes. I trust they will unfold with love and wisdom."*
- If a specific talent or ability comes to mind, imagine yourself using it joyfully and confidently.

Seal the Activation
- Take a deep breath and imagine weaving this golden light into your energy field, like a shining thread connecting your past, present and future selves.
- Whisper: *"The wisdom of my soul awakens gently and guides me now."*

Return and Reflect
- Open your eyes slowly and write down any impressions, ideas or emotions that came to you. Even if they seem small or unclear, trust they are the first stirrings of your ancient gifts reawakening.
- Say aloud: *"I honour the gifts I have carried through time. I awaken them now with love, sharing them for the highest good."*

NOTES:

Soul Spark

Awakening Sacred Gifts

Take a quiet moment to reflect after your Soul Gift Activation Ritual. Let your words flow freely, without judgment. This is your sacred space to dream, to declare and to weave with the first whispers that rise from your intentions.

What gift feels most natural to me, as if I have always known it?
(What do I do with ease, even without formal learning?)

What am I most drawn to exploring right now?
(What excites me or feels magnetic, even if I don't understand why?)

What lesson has a challenging soul relationship taught me?
(How has this connection pushed me to grow stronger, wiser or more compassionate?)

How can I begin living one of my soul gifts this week?
(What simple action could honour and strengthen it today?)

When you are finished, place your hand over your heart and repeat the affirmation

I honour the gifts I have carried through time. I awaken them now with love, sharing them for the highest good.

Sacred Notes
Space to Weave your Soul Threads

Chapter 7:
Woven Wholeness:
Living as the Soul You Are

Living as a Whole Being

Every thread of your soul's journey - every joy, lesson, challenge and healing - has brought you to this moment. Woven wholeness is not about becoming perfect or striving for a distant spiritual ideal; it is about embracing all that you are, integrating every experience and living from the truth of your Eternal Self.

When you live as the soul you are, there is a quiet sense of alignment. Life may not always be easy, but you begin to trust its flow. Choices feel guided rather than forced and you feel connected to something greater - not outside of you, but within you.

Peace begins to rise when you stop trying to fix yourself and start honouring the weaving that already exists. You realise that every thread - even the messy, tangled ones - is part of your unique pattern.

What it Means to Be Woven Whole

Being woven whole does not mean you never feel sadness, fear or doubt. It means you accept those feelings as part of your tapestry, without letting them define you.

When you embrace every part of yourself, you begin to:

- Honour all that you have been and all that you are becoming.
- Respond with compassion rather than reaction.
- Recognise old patterns without allowing them to control you.
- Live in a way that feels authentic, peaceful and guided by love.

Woven wholeness is not about becoming more; it is about remembering that you have always been whole.

Gathering All the Threads

Think of your life as a weaving made of many threads - past lives, soul connections, karmic lessons and ancient gifts. Some threads are golden and bright, representing joy and love. Others are darker, carrying the weight of challenges and wounds.

Wholeness comes when you stop rejecting any part of your weaving. Even the darker threads belong. They have shaped you, taught you and made the brighter ones shine more vividly.

When you embrace every part of your story, you feel a soft peace - a sense that nothing has been wasted. Every experience, no matter how painful, has contributed to the soul you are becoming.

Trusting the Wisdom of Your Journey

There was a time when I questioned certain choices, wondering if I had taken the "wrong path." But looking back, I see how every detour brought wisdom. Even the mistakes led me to people I needed to meet or lessons I needed to learn.

When you view life through the soul's eyes, there are no wasted experiences. Everything, even the difficult chapters, is part of the greater weaving. The Eternal Self does not judge these moments as good or bad; it simply honours them as part of the whole.

The Courage to Integrate

True integration takes courage. It means sitting with the parts of yourself you once tried to hide, forgiving yourself for old mistakes and accepting that you are not defined by your past.

It is easy to love the parts of yourself that feel light and joyful. The real work is in loving the parts that feel heavy - the mistakes, the regrets, the moments you wish you could change.

Wholeness is born when you can look at those parts and say: *"You belong. You are part of me, and I honour what you taught me."*

Living in Alignment with the Soul

Living soul-aligned does not require a dramatic life change. It begins with simple, daily choices:
- Listening inward before making decisions, asking, *"Does this feel expansive or heavy?"*
- Following what feels true, even if it doesn't make sense to others.
- Speaking and acting with integrity, even in small ways.
- Allowing joy without guilt, as joy itself is healing.
- Trusting the timing of your life, knowing your soul is guiding you.

Every time you choose love over fear, truth over avoidance, or peace over conflict, you strengthen the golden threads in your life's tapestry.

The Quiet Shifts that Change Everything

Some of the most profound changes happen quietly. You may notice you respond differently to old triggers or choose rest instead of pushing through exhaustion.

These small shifts are signs that you are living more as your Eternal Self - guided not by old patterns, but by the wisdom you have gathered across lifetimes

The Power of Presence

Woven wholeness is also about being present. Too often we live in the past, caught in regret or in the future, worrying about what's to come. But your soul exists in the now.

When you slow down, breathe and fully experience the present moment, you open the door to deeper guidance. The Eternal Self speaks most clearly in stillness - in quiet moments where nothing needs to be achieved, only felt.

The Moment I Truly Felt Whole

There was a day - ordinary in every way - when I sat quietly with a cup of tea, watching sunlight filter through the trees. Nothing special was happening, but I felt a wave of peace wash over me.

It was a sense of quiet knowing: *I am exactly where I am meant to be. Everything has led me here.*

That is woven wholeness - not a dramatic spiritual awakening, but a deep, grounded acceptance of who you are, here and now.

The Ripple Effect of Living Whole

When you live as the soul you are, your presence itself becomes healing. You do not need to preach, teach or convince anyone of anything. People feel it in how you move through the world - in your calmness, kindness and quiet strength.

Your peace ripples outward, influencing others in ways you may never fully see. Every loving choice, every moment of alignment, weaves light into the collective tapestry.

Returning When You Forget

There will be days when you feel far from this wholeness. That is part of being human. But even in those moments, you can return to yourself by pausing, breathing and remembering: *You are already whole. You have never left your soul.*

The journey of wholeness is not about staying perfectly aligned every day; it is about remembering and returning, again and again, with love.

The Weaving of Wholeness

Imagine your soul as a tapestry stretching across lifetimes. Every thread - bright or dark, smooth or knotted - belongs. Together they create a design far more beautiful than any single piece alone.

When you honour all the threads - the joys, the sorrows, the lessons and the love - your life begins to feel whole. You realise that nothing has been wasted and everything you are carries meaning.

The more you live from this truth, the more your tapestry glows - shimmering with the golden light of acceptance, love and soul wisdom.

Your Next Step

Take a moment to read and connect with the Affirmation Thread. Let it remind you that you are already whole, already living the wisdom of your soul with every loving choice you make.

When you feel ready, move to the Thread Ritual - The Weaving Wholeness, where you will consciously honour the life you have woven and set the intention to continue living fully as the soul you truly are.

Affirmation

I AM ETERNAL,

WHOLE AND WOVEN FROM EVERY LIFETIME INTO ONE.

MY SOUL REMEMBERS ALL THAT I HAVE BEEN.

I TRUST THE GOLDEN THREADS THAT WEAVE ME WHOLE.

I HONOUR EVERY EXPERIENCE THAT SHAPED ME

AND I LIVE AS THE SACRED THREAD I AM.

Thread Ritual
The Weaving of Wholeness

Purpose
To integrate all parts of yourself and embody the truth of who you are, living fully as your soul in this lifetime.

Prepare Your Space
- Sit somewhere quiet where you feel calm and undisturbed.
- Light a candle or place an object that represents wholeness to you - a crystal, a feather or even a simple stone.
- Take three slow breaths, letting your body relax.

Ground Yourself into the Present
- Close your eyes and imagine roots growing from your feet deep into the earth.
- With each breath, feel steady, safe and held.
- Whisper: *"I am safe. I am ready to welcome every part of me home."*

Call Home Every Thread
- Visualise a great golden tapestry before you, shimmering with threads of every colour.
- Each thread represents a part of you - your joys, wounds, strengths, past lives and soul gifts.
- See the loose threads gently weaving back into place, creating a single, radiant fabric.
- Whisper: *"I welcome every part of me. I am whole. I am love."*

Align with Your Soul
- Place your hands on your heart. Feel its steady rhythm.
- Say softly: *"Guide me to live as the soul I truly am. May my thoughts, words and actions reflect my truth and love."*
- Sit for a few moments, feeling calm alignment settle through your body.

Seal the Weave
- Imagine golden light wrapping gently around you, holding all of you together in harmony.
- Whisper: *"I am the weaving of all I have been and all I will become. I live now as the soul I truly am."*

Return and Reflect
- Open your eyes and write down how you feel or any insights that arose.
- Notice any sense of peace, clarity or lightness as you move through your day.

NOTES:

Soul Spark
Golden Thread Reflections

Take a quiet moment to reflect after The Weaving of Wholeness Ritual. Let your words flow freely, without judgment. This is your sacred space to dream, to declare and to weave with the first whispers that rise from your intentions.

What parts of me have I struggled to accept?
(What would happen if I welcomed them home with love?)

Where in my life do I feel most aligned with my soul?
(What moments make me feel authentic, peaceful and whole?)

What simple daily action could help me live more as my true self?
(What small step could I take to honour my soul's wisdom today?)

If I trusted I am already whole, how would my life feel different?
(What would change in how I speak, act or choose?)

When you are finished, place your hand over your heart and repeat the affirmation

I am whole. I am the weaving of all I have been and all I will become. I live now as the soul I truly am.

Sacred Notes
Space to Weave your Soul Threads

Part IV: The Continuing Thread

Chapter 8:
Closing Reflection:
Weaving Your Own Sacred Thread

The Journey You Have Walked

As you turn these final pages, pause and breathe. You have travelled through lifetimes in these chapters - not only the ones written in words, but the ones remembered in the quiet moments of reflection, in the rituals you honoured and in the memories your soul stirred awake.

You have looked into the timeless nature of your Eternal Self, explored the echoes of past lives, healed karmic threads, honoured sacred agreements, remembered soul connections, reawakened ancient gifts and embraced your wholeness.

Each step has been a thread, woven into the greater tapestry of your soul's remembrance. Some threads have felt soft and golden, glowing with love and joy. Others may have been heavier, carrying lessons, release or healing. Yet all belong.

And now, the weaving continues in your hands.

What It Means to Weave Your Own Sacred Thread

To weave your own sacred thread is to live with intention. It is the choice to bring all that you have remembered into every breath, every action and every relationship.

This is no longer just a journey of reflection, but a way of life - one where every moment becomes an opportunity to embody your soul.

Your sacred thread is uniquely yours. No one else can weave it for you. It is made of:
- Wisdom of lifetimes.
- Love you have given and received.
- Lessons you have learned through challenge and grace.
- Soul gifts you choose to share.

When you live this way, you are not just remembering; you are actively creating the story your soul came here to write. You are no longer simply walking through life; you are weaving it - choice by choice, thought by thought, thread by thread.

The Weaving Continues Beyond These Pages

This book may be complete, but your soul's weaving is endless. Each day you are adding new threads - some bright with joy, some softer with healing, some strong with resilience. All are sacred.

There will still be challenges, but now you hold a deeper understanding: every experience, no matter how tangled or frayed, can be woven into something meaningful.

Even when the pattern does not make sense in the moment, trust that the Eternal Self sees the whole design. The very threads you once thought were mistakes may, in time, reveal themselves as turning points of wisdom.

You are no longer just a passenger in life's unfolding - you are the weaver. Your hands hold the threads; your choices guide the pattern.

The Soul's Gentle Reminders

As you step forward, remember:
- Trust your inner knowing. Your soul speaks quietly but clearly when you listen.
- Honour what you feel drawn to. What excites or soothes you is often a sign of alignment.
- Use your gifts. No act of love or creativity is too small; every expression matters.
- Release what no longer serves you. Some threads are meant to fall away so new ones can be woven.
- Choose love over fear. This is the strongest golden thread you can weave into your life.

Living Your Sacred Thread Daily

You do not need to change everything at once. Your sacred thread is woven through small, conscious acts:
- Taking a mindful breath before speaking.
- Offering kindness when you could choose judgment.
- Sitting in stillness and listening to your soul's whispers.
- Following through on the things that light you up inside.
- Pausing to be grateful for the simple, sacred moments - a sunrise, a shared smile, a quiet cup of tea.

Each of these is a thread, strengthening the fabric of your life and deepening your connection to your Eternal Self. Over time, these quiet moments of presence become golden strands that transform how you experience everything.

The Simple Moments of Soul Alignment

Some of the most soul-aligned moments are not grand or extraordinary - they are the quietest ones.

For me, some of the clearest moments of connection have been as simple as sitting with my hands wrapped around a warm cup of tea, feeling the morning sun on my skin. Or pausing in the middle of a busy day to place my hands over my heart, breathing slowly and whispering, "I am here. I am whole."

There was a time when I thought living soulfully meant doing something big or world-changing. Now I know it is the quiet choices, repeated daily, that weave the strongest golden threads.

Your Soul's Legacy

The sacred thread you weave in this lifetime is not just for you - it is for those who come after you and for the collective soul of humanity. Every choice you make, every moment of love, forgiveness or courage, is a golden thread added to the greater tapestry of life.

Each act of kindness, no matter how small, sends ripples outward. A gentle word spoken in compassion, a smile offered to a stranger, a moment of patience when you could have reacted with anger - these seem like tiny threads, but together they weave powerful change. You may never fully see how far your threads stretch, but they do.

The words you speak, the love you share, the healing you offer - it all continues beyond you, touching lives in ways you may never know. A kind gesture may inspire someone else to act with love, which in turn touches another life and another. In this way, your soul's weaving expands far beyond your own story.

Some of the greatest legacies are not measured by achievements or recognition but by the quiet ways a soul has shifted the energy of the world. Choosing love in a moment of fear, offering understanding instead of judgment, forgiving yourself when it would be easier to hold on to guilt - these are acts of soul weaving.

And this weaving does not end when this life does. One day, when your soul chooses another life, you will pick up these same threads again, continuing to weave with even more wisdom and grace. Every golden strand you weave now will guide your future self, just as the gifts and lessons you carry today were woven long ago.

Your choices now become the foundation of future lives. Every time you choose love over fear, every time you honour your soul gifts, every time you heal an old karmic pattern, you lighten the threads not only for yourself but for the generations of souls who will walk after you.

In this way, you are not only weaving your life - you are contributing to the great collective tapestry of all souls. The love you embody now strengthens the golden threads for everyone, reminding us all of what we truly are: eternal, interconnected and made of light.

So, when you doubt the impact of your journey, remember this: your soul's legacy is already being written with every conscious choice. Every thread matters. Every act of love matters. And long after this life has passed, your weaving will continue to shine, guiding others - and guiding you - home to the Eternal Self again and again.

A Gentle Closing Vision

If you wish, close your eyes for a moment and imagine this:

You are sitting before a great Loom of Light, your hands holding a shimmering golden thread. Every memory, lesson and act of love you have ever given or received glows within it.

You take this thread and weave it into the greater tapestry of your soul. Some threads are bright and glowing, some soft and quiet but all are beautiful.

The loom hums softly as you continue weaving - not just for yourself, but for all souls connected to you. Every choice you make, every act of love you give, ripples through this sacred weaving, adding more light to the collective tapestry of all life.

And as you weave, you feel the truth rise gently in your heart: *You are not just part of the tapestry. You are both the weaver and the thread.*

Your Next Step

Take a moment to read and connect with the Affirmation Thread. Let it remind you that you are the weaver of your sacred thread and that every choice, no matter how small, is part of your soul's greater tapestry.

When you feel ready, move to the Thread Ritual - Integrating Your Sacred Thread, where you will consciously honour all the threads you have gathered and set the intention to continue living fully as the soul you truly are.

Your weaving continues, always.

Affirmation

I AM THE WEAVER OF MY SACRED THREAD.

EVERY LIFETIME, EVERY LESSON

EVERY SOUL CONNECTION LIVES WITHIN ME.

I HONOUR MY GIFTS, EMBRACE MY WHOLENESS

AND WEAVE MY LIFE NOW WITH LOVE,

WISDOM AND LIGHT.

Thread Ritual
Integrating Your Sacred Thread

Purpose
To consciously integrate everything you have remembered and step forward as the weaver of your own sacred life, aligning with love, wisdom and wholeness.

Prepare Your Space
- Sit somewhere quiet where you can reflect without distraction.
- Light a candle or hold something symbolic - a piece of thread, ribbon or a crystal that feels like it holds your energy.
- Take a few deep breaths, allowing your body to settle.

Weaving Begins
- Close your eyes and visualise a great loom before you, glowing with golden light.
- See all the threads of your journey - past lives, soul lessons, healing, gifts and connections - stretching out before you.
- Whisper: *"Every thread of my soul is sacred. I welcome it all into the weaving of who I am."*

Weave With Intention
- Imagine taking these threads into your hands, weaving them together with love.
- As you weave, think of how you want to live moving forward.
- Whisper or think of the qualities you wish to weave: *"I weave love... I weave courage... I weave joy... I weave truth..."*
- Continue until you feel the tapestry glow brighter, whole and complete.

Seal the Weaving
- Place your hands over your heart and say softly: *"I am the weaver of my sacred thread. I live now as the soul I truly am - whole, eternal and guided by love."*

Return and Reflect
- Open your eyes gently.
- If you feel called, write down what you felt or any words, images or guidance that came through.
- Keep your symbolic item (thread, ribbon or crystal) as a reminder of this new beginning.

NOTES:

Soul Spark
Carrying the Thread Forward

Take a quiet moment to reflect after your Integrating Your Sacred Thread Ritual. Let your words flow freely, without judgment. This is your sacred space to dream, to declare and to weave with the first whispers that rise from your intentions.

What threads from my past feel most important to carry forward?
(What wisdom, gifts or lessons do I want to keep weaving into my life?)

What new threads do I want to weave into my story now?
(What qualities - love, courage, joy, peace - do I choose to strengthen from this day forward?)

What does living as my whole, soul-aligned self look and feel like?
(Describe a moment, vision or way of being that feels true to my Eternal Self.)

How can I honour my sacred thread each day?
(What simple daily action or mindset will keep me aligned with who I truly am?)

When you are finished, place your hand over your heart and repeat the affirmation

I am the weaver of my sacred thread. I live now as the soul I truly am - whole, eternal and guided by love.

Sacred Notes

Space to Weave your Soul Threads

Notes

Notes

Thank you for walking this sacred journey with me through *Sacred Threads*.

I hope these pages have offered you insight, healing and a deeper remembrance of who you truly are. Every reflection you write, every ritual you honour and every thread you weave back into your heart is part of your soul's unfolding story.

Trust what your soul remembers. Embrace the lessons with love and honour the timeless wisdom within you.

I am deeply grateful for your time, energy and presence. If this book has touched you or reawakened something within, I would love to hear about your experience. Your reflections and stories are part of this sacred weaving too.

May your path continue to unfold with wisdom, love and golden threads of light guiding your way.

Share Your Journey
I would love to hear from you!
Tag me online or email me your reflections and favourite moments from *Sacred Threads*. Your story may inspire another soul to remember their own sacred thread.

THESACREDSPACEPRESS.COM

PUBLISHED WORLDWIDE

MMXXV

ISBN 978-1-7640433-2-8

9 781764 043328

www.ingramcontent.com/pod-product-compliance
Lightning Source LLC
Chambersburg PA
CBHW040043100526
44583CB00027BA/3260